I0558936

TRINITY WALK

TO

Spiritual
Mental
Physical

SELF- LOVE

This journal is to share my trinity walk to self-love and different techniques that helped me. In the following chapters, I will teach and guide you in diverse ways to give, receive, and set boundaries to start you on your successful journey. It is written in the order that helped me while on my path to healing, and if you decide to follow my path, you can change the order to accommodate you.

Another way to navigate this path is by adding a trustworthy friend who is nonjudgmental and will hold you accountable. You want someone you can trust with your emotions. There will be times when you have to be brutally honest with yourself, and you may want to vent to someone; just make sure they are trustworthy. If you cannot trust a friend, try doing daily journaling, find a therapist, or trust God, because we know He will never turn His back on us or tell our business. I actually had two riders that I trusted with my process: my friends Kendra M. and Cynthia U. are the two who understood the assignment and the importance of me healing from all the heartbreaks that I experienced. They held me accountable and encouraged me when I wanted to give up, helped and motivated me to stay focused so that I could help you. My prayer while you are on your journey is that you learn to become the best version of yourself by seeing yourself through your own eyes as the beautiful being God created you to be.

Sincerely,

Coach Ni

Introduction

My name is Niesha Knox. I was born in East Chicago, Indiana, but raised in Gary, Indiana. I was the only daughter of three and considered the responsible one. I decided to write this journal to share my testimony in hopes of helping others navigate or start their healing through self-love. If you are reading this journal, that means you are interested in discovering your higher self. Feeling lost and lonely is what prompted my journey. I lost my father in 2021 and chose not to grieve him because I thought if I didn't acknowledge it, then it wasn't real. In fact, I was unknowingly grieving him in an unhealthy way that showed through my outward appearance. I lost a lot of weight due to worrying about him while he was sick and during his transition. My heart was shattered, and I kept saying, "What am I supposed to do now?" I was looking for someone to just take the wheel, but I was considered the strong one, so I didn't get my cup filled. Now, don't get me wrong, my Aunt Annie and a few other people checked on me heavily during and after, but they still couldn't fill my cup because I didn't open up and be truthful about my pain. I was so used to doing it on my own and being forgotten about that I learned how to not wear my emotions on my face or sleeve. The real truth is that the "strong" ones are very sensitive and hold back tears until we find a safe place to let it out. One year later, I remarried my first husband after 10 years, thinking my life was finally turning around. Yup, that was just a test because 11 months later, I filed for divorce, and once again, I took that pain and went inward. Except this time, I decided not to give him any of my emotions, and on the outside, I looked good. I was hurt, but I had to continue acting strong and went through it silently. A couple of months later, my friend Vanda Cook passed away, and in that same month, it seemed like I was being attacked left and right. Her death was the final straw, and I broke down like a child. I felt like my breath was snatched out of me, and I had no energy left to give anyone. God broke me all the way down and made me face the true reality that I had been so used to running from. It was like a nightmare that I couldn't wake up from. I had to go inward so deeply to heal childhood trauma, and I cried for months. When I left the house, I would put on a happy face, but when I came home, I had to face each issue and speak to it to heal from it. However, God was doing a new thing and didn't let me go through this alone. My sons prayed, comforted and spoke life over me during those dark hours. He also blessed me with my friend Vanda's family, especially her Aunt Cassandra and our mutual friend Serita. These groups of people gave me a safe place to grieve and to be vulnerable without feeling judged. This was the beginning of my spiritual and mental phase of the trinity walk to self-love. Physical fitness was my very first step in my healing journey. I've been personal training for years, and my mission was to help women regain their power back through physical fitness. Years later, I decided to add spiritual and mental to my healing and self-love. Adding spiritual, mental, and physical together produced trinity of fitness, which gave me the recipe to create Trinity Walk to Self-Love.

Before we jump into the journal, let's look at the meanings of love
:

1. What does love look like in the Spiritual realm? 1 Corinthians 13:4-8 NIV: Love is patient, love is kind. It does not envy, it does not boast, it is not proud. It does not dishonor others; it is not self-seeking; it is not easily angered; it keeps no record of wrongs. Love does not delight in evil but rejoices with the truth. It always protects, always trusts, always hopes, always perseveres. Love never fails."

2. What does love look like in the Physical? Love in the physical realm is to have an intense feeling of deep affection, an immense pleasure in something. Love in the 3D realm (human) can be conditional. This type of love can show sympathy but not empathy. Love in the Physical comes with stipulations and rules (for example, If we are married or in a relationship, I love you, but as soon as we divorce or separate, the love seems to never exist.)

3. What is Self-Love? The book of Ephesians 5:29 says, "No one ever hated his own flesh, but nourish and cherishes it, just as the Lord does the church." If that is true, why must we teach or learn self-love? The world has forgotten all about the basic laws, but instead, it is driven by the laws of man. We no longer look in the mirror to see our true selves; we just look straight ahead at everything we idolize and start considering that love. Then, when the doors are closed, lights off, lace fronts and lashes off, and suction suits peeled off, we are then sitting in our true timeline, which is depression and anxiety. We are depressed and cannot get over anxiety because we never poured into ourselves. The root of this can be traced back to our ancestors and the generational curses placed on our bloodlines. We will get into that at another time in another book but understand that we live in a time where selfishness, greed, and conditional love drive our world.

Chapter 1

Trinity of Fitness

Spiritual, Mental and Physical Fitness

Spiritual, Mental, and Physical Fitness are the beginning stages of understanding yourself. I strongly believe this to be true because it is the trinity of self-love. It reminds me of the divine Trinity: The Father, Son, and Holy Spirit. You cannot have one without the other; there is no way you can gain access to the heavens and blessings without the other. The trinity of fitness is the same way. You cannot access your higher self fully without tapping into and strengthening each group. Now, let us define each fitness.

<u>What does each fitness look like when dealing with Self-love?</u>

1. **Spiritual Fitness** - If we are created in God's image, and God is Love, then we should be operating and glowing with love. Spiritual love is a fruit of the Holy Spirit and how God expects us to live. This type of love is not jealous, boastful, angry, envious, or filled with hatred or self-sabotage. But it is filled with Galatians 5:22-23: "But the fruit of the Spirit is love, joy, peace, forbearance, kindness, goodness, faithfulness, gentleness and self-control." When operating in love, you allow yourself to vibrate in your higher self on the highest frequency, also known as the highest gift of God: Love. This will allow you to have patience and show kindness to yourself and others.

2. **Mental Fitness** - We tend to look at everything in the physical world first instead of the spiritual. This creates illusions in our minds of anxiety, depression, and confusion because we manifest what we create mentally. That is why it is especially important to build healthy boundaries and communicate our true feelings so we can break down illusions and live in truth. Training your mind will allow you to see things for what they are instead of what they seem. Paul says in 1 Corinthians 2:10, "The Spirit searches all things, even the deep things of God." This ties into Spiritual fitness; once you understand the fitness trinity, life becomes less perplexing. I do need you to understand that this can cause confusion because sometimes the underlying issues may be mental health issues, and you may need clinical help to balance your mind. So, be sure to seek help if needed.

3. *__Physical Fitness__* - Through physical fitness, you start to realize much more about yourself when you are pressured to perform. As a personal trainer, it is important to explain to clients not to look at fitness as an act of punishment but to see it as an act of love that will nourish your mind, body, and soul. This fitness is usually the first step for most as they start their self-love journey. This started my process of finding and seeking my higher self. It pushed me to look outside at the illusions I created or were handed down through generational curses. I chose to re-create the illusions by seeking God (truth). As I built my outside to look good, I began to self-reflect and noticed that my insides did not feel or look like the outward man, so I decided to search for healing to build my mental and spiritual man. Are you ready to apply the Trinity of Self-Love to your life?

__Self-Reflections:__
1.Which fitness have you started, or will you start?
2.What actions can you take now to prepare you for your self-love journey?
3.How do you define self-love?

In the next chapters, I will share the barriers that were blocking me and how I overcame them during my healing journey to self-love.

Chapter 2

Gratitude

1 Thessalonians 5:18 In Everything Give Thanks

Gratitude is giving thanks and appreciation for things that are good and bad. You ask, "Why would I give thanks and appreciation for the bad things I had to endure?" Well, my friend, this is a major key to a successful Self-Love journey. During your healing process, your perception of the word and feeling of "bad" will change greatly. Bad things are pivotal points in our lives to make us stronger, confident, and understand boundaries. 1 Thessalonians 5 states, "In everything give thanks," and we must trust God and accept that things happen for reasons unknown to us. Accepting that will eliminate the confusion created by the illusions built around the "what, why, when, and how" questions. Trusting in the Most High will give you the comfort you need while going through trials and tribulations. Showing gratitude to God should start your day, but I need you to also understand that you have to give thanks to yourself. You can give God all the praise and thanks, and your inner self still feels unworthy and bruised.

This is just an illusion we feed into because we don't give ourselves credit and acknowledge our own strength and worthiness. I struggled for years with the unworthy feeling of "I didn't do anything to be proud of" or "I am not good enough or deserving enough to be congratulated." I would show gratitude to God and still feel like I had to take several backseats in the nosebleed section because I wasn't important. Those are the lies the enemy planted in my mind, and it caused me to self-sabotage.

Healing starts when you tell yourself, "Congratulations, thank you, I love you, you are worthy, and you have a purpose here in this world." You must remain grateful for all things and, most importantly, give yourselves a big hug, pat on the back, and say thank you because you did the work and fought the good fight.

Self- Reflection:
1. Start your mornings giving thanks to the Most High, and then look in the mirror and say to yourself, "Thank you for staying strong."
2. Create a journal to list out all the things you owe gratitude to.
3. Practice incorporating gratitude into your daily routine.

Chapter 3

Pouring into Yourself

Galatians 5:22-23(NIV) But the fruit of the Spirit is love, joy, peace, forbearance, kindness, goodness, faithfulness, gentleness and self-control. Against such things there is no law.

As a single mom of two teenage boys, the only daughter, and considered the responsible one of the family, I find myself burned out trying to be the mom, daughter, sister, friend, employee, healer, protector, etc., to everyone and not taking the time out to nurture my three areas of fitness as we talked about. This caused me to feel drained because I gave all my energy and poured it into everyone's cup to help them feel better, but my return was the feeling of being depleted. You must remember: Self-love is not selfish; it is a way to ground your spiritual and mental to balance your overall physical fitness. Your spiritual self begins to call out and yearn for energy to keep you balanced with the Divine, and your mental fitness will become more focused to allow clear communication with your intuition. You cannot be stable mentally without an aura recharge. Once your battery is 100%, you can begin to pour into others, but this time with boundaries on how much and to whom you give your energy. I see myself as the power company and friends, family, or whoever requires my energy as the customer. I, the power company, will never run out of energy because I produce it by grounding myself. When people do not pay their bills, their services become disconnected. I supply the customers with a package plan called an "Energy Pull Limit." Once they connect to me, my job is to allow them to plug in, and my spirit or intuition will notify me when they have reached their "Energy Pull Limit," and services will then be disconnected with love. We have to remember that our role is to allow God to show Himself through us by love, and in return, the person seeking energy will seek God to get their ever-lasting water that Jesus spoke about in John 4:13-14. When you pour into yourself, you should, with no hesitation, handle yourself with gentleness.

Gentleness is the quality of being kind, tender, or mild-mannered; it is a softness of oneself, not to be confused as weak but seen as strong. Being able to work out of your masculine and feminine energy in a cohesive way will allow you to stand in your power and exude strength. Paul speaks of walking worthy of the calling which you were called, with lowliness and gentleness (Ephesians 4:1-3). The takeaway from this is what my father always told me: "Be who you are and love yourself." Reflect back on your life and ask yourself, "Am I loving myself?"

Self- Reflection:

1. What are ways you can pour into yourself?
2. Where do you lack boundaries?
3. What steps can you take to ensure you are putting self-first in the future?

Chapter 4

Learning the Difference Between Sin- Less and Sinless

I heard this saying: "If it is BORN by the spirit, it must be GOVERNED by the spirit."

This chapter deals with our spiritual fitness and how to overcome blockages. During my self-love journey, spiritual fitness was my hardest fitness challenge. I began to get in my head that God will never forgive me, and I am not good enough for God to use me. I self-doubted everything when it came to doing God's work. Then I received the words from Ephesians 4:9-10 (NIV) (What does "he ascended" mean except that he also descended to the lower, earthly regions? He who descended is the very one who ascended higher than all the heavens to fill the whole universe). Then the words sin-less came to mind. I remember my old Pastor said sin-less to strive to become sinless. This helped me understand that the only man on this earth who had no sin was Jesus, so why am I pressuring myself to be someone I am not? Instead, I should strive to be like Him and challenge myself every day to become sinless. Then, I stopped doubting God's visions; instead, I would take it back to Him in conversation and ask for clarity. Remember, if God created you, then you must understand that His love for you is unconditional. No matter what you do, God will still use you as His vessel to get the job done. Remember, Paul was Saul before God used him.

Self- Reflection:

1. What are your spiritual blockages?
2. Why do you feel they are blockages?
3. What steps should you take to prevent these blockages from a affecting your future?

Chapter 5

Receiving Love and Blessings

Psalm 23:5 (NIV) You prepare a table before me in the presence of my enemies. You anoint my head with oil; my cup overflows.

Most people are better givers than receivers, and it is not a terrible thing, but God wants us to receive as well. I have always been a giver, and I can count on my right hand the number of people in my life who have genuinely given to me without my asking or without looking for something in return. Even if someone tried to bless me, I found a way to either give it back or just not accept it. As a child, I always had a genuine love inside of me and would not accept gifts humbly because I always felt there was someone else who needed it more than me. This behavior really worried my father because, given the type of humility and love I showed others, he knew people would take advantage of me. My father began teaching me and instilling values that would guide me in his absence. He drilled into my head, "Woogie" (my nickname), remember to always respect the next man or woman, always reach back, and give what you can without going broke. Well, I did everything he told me except for the give without going broke part. I gave and gave until I was without and standing in front of God crying, "Please God, help me!" because I had nothing for myself. God came through, and I would do it all over again because my heart was so big and all I wanted to do in life was to help anyone in need. I even put up with people thinking they were using me, but the whole time they did not know I operated from an unhealed, unconditionally loving place. Unhealed meaning, I had no boundaries, I allowed people to come and go, take, disrespect, and I dealt with severe low self-esteem. One day, I said enough, put my foot down, established boundaries, and started operating on a higher frequency. This is when God started to pour into me because he saw I was ready to receive. It was in those dark moments when God taught me how to receive love and blessings. When everyone turned their back on me, talked about me, made fun of my shortcomings, played in my face, and disrespected me for the last time, that's when God stepped in and picked me up in their face, sat me at a table where they could only see the different appetizers and entrees I was eating. He set me up high so my enemies could only look up to see me, and then He did the most shocking thing ever: He re-introduced me with a new name, voice, speech, glow, and swag. In those moments, I got to understand what Psalm 23:5 meant. He hid me in plain sight and allowed me to be revealed at the right time because I finally chose me, and in choosing me, I learned to receive love the way I knew I deserved it. I learned that I am the blessing that comes into people's lives, and God chose me to be the vessel to help guide his people through my gift of love. Paul said it best in Romans 11:22 (NIV) Consider therefore the kindness and sternness of God: sternness to those who fell, but kindness to you, provided that you continue in his kindness. Because I chose to operate in my gift of love and kindness, God has blessed me with everything I prayed for because He knew I was ready, and I turned away from living a Self-Sabotage life to living a Self-Loved life. Are you a giver who is now ready to learn to receive?

Self- Reflection:

1. Are you a giver or a receiver?
2. What boundaries are you going to establish to allow yourself to be the receiver?
3. How will you prepare yourself not to block Love and Blessings in the future?

Chapter 6

Self-Control

Learning Gray Areas

Self-control is the ability to control your emotions and desires or the expression in your behavior, especially in difficult situations. Being able to control yourself under pressure or during spiritual warfare is a gift. I practiced self-control for years and I am just learning to master it but be mindful: each season of your life will present more tricky situations, and you may have to revise your self-control tactics to fit those scenarios. I had to attend therapy, and my therapist, Mrs. Hughs, taught me about a gray area. I habitually went from 0 to 100 and from 100 to 0 quickly. If you look at it, I was a modern-day Dr. Jekyll and Mr. Hyde, which is scary any way you look at it. When I used to get angry, I felt like I was turning into the Hulk. I would get back spasms and veins popping out of the side of my neck and forehead, then I lost control. After I settled down and looked around, I thought, "Dang, I'm going to jail today" because I had broken tables, busted lips, and destroyed property, and everyone was looking at me as if I had lost my mind. I learned that the back spasms were my cue to stop, step back, adjust my thinking, and remove myself from those situations. So, instead of getting to 100, that gray area stopped me at 20, and I was able to step back, assess the situation, and take a more reasonable approach. Learning to remove myself from situations that no longer served me was the key that I learned during my journey. Self-control is not easy, but you have to remember that you are in control at all times. Patience and practice are the answers to this solution.

Self- Reflection:

1. Do you have a gray area?
2. What areas of your life should be reassessed to prevent you from losing control of your emotions?
3. How will you prepare yourself to maintain control in difficult situations in the future?

Chapter 7

Accountability

Hebrews 4:13 (NIV) Nothing in all creation is hidden from God's sight. Everything is uncovered and laid bare before the eyes of him to whom we must give account.

Accountability is an obligation or willingness to accept responsibility for one's actions. Romans 14:12 (NIV) "we all will give an account of ourselves to God." As far as I can remember, I have always held myself to a higher standard of judgment, meaning I held myself accountable for everything, even if I knew it was not my fault. I felt the need to take accountability for others' actions because I felt bad for them. Meanwhile, the people who hurt me are prancing around, living their best lives, while I am dwelling on the hurt from the convictions that were theirs to carry. During my self-love journey, I had to reflect back on all the shame or disappointments I felt over the years about my actions. While reflecting, I realized that all the guilt, shame, and disappointment had nothing to do with me. I realized I was carrying everyone else's problems that they projected onto me. I had to account for my part, understand how that affected my emotions, and discard the rest. It's like I went into my closet to do spring cleaning, kept what served me, packed up the items that did not serve me, and returned them to the sender. I had to address each item and send the item back to the manufacturing company that produced that faulty material, and in return, I reclaimed all my power and energy. Once I called all my power and energy back, I did my mental and emotional makeover and clothed myself with a policy that reads, "I do not accept any drama, let me borrow, disrespect, negativity, trauma bonding, energy stealing, 'I was going to do,' 'I really do love you but,' 'I can't stop thinking about us,' 'Can I get one more chance,' or love bombing of any kind." This caused a heavy aroma of peace to fill my space because now when people see me and look me up and down to read my policy, they turn and go the other way. When you start to take accountability for your actions, God will then be able to shift things in your life, and He will protect you by heightening your intuition to guide your steps in your next season. Your intuition will then know whom to trust and not trust. Are you taking accountability for your actions and emotions?

Self- Reflection:

1. What does accountability look like for you?
2. Reflect back on a situation when you didn't take accountability for your actions.
3. Do you think that situation caused you to self-sabotage or provoke unnecessary emotions?
4. How will you practice accountability in the future?

Chapter 8

Protecting Your Energy

2 Corinthians Chapter 12: 10 (TPT)- For my weakness becomes a portal to God's power.

Friends let's talk about the importance of energy and why we should protect it at all costs. I want to explain spiritual energy and what it means to us. What is energy? Energy simply means the ability to work. If you look at it spiritually, spiritual energy is energy that is generated within yourself. You have to treat energy like currency. Currency flows in and out; no matter how you look at it, whether rich or poor, the currency will always flow. Some people can manipulate ways to get currency, hoard it, give it away, and mistreat it. But, in order for your currency to grow and mature, you have to treat it right by investing, wise spending, and not being ruled by it. The same goes for your energy. If you want to get and stay in a positive energy and stay at a high vibration, you have to protect it. Believe it or not, some people are sent into our lives to kill our joy, steal our energy, and destroy the pathway to our blessings. John 10:10 (NIV) says, "The thief comes only to steal, kill, and destroy." This is why it is important to keep open communication with the Divine, because, as I talked about in chapter 7 about trusting your intuition, God will show you clearly who is sent by Him and who is sent by the enemy. You have to invest your energy in something that will keep your spiritual, mental, and physical- self vibrating higher than the enemy's frequency. You cannot hoard your energy because God made us to see the beauty in each other and to be a testimony for others. He wants us to help each other, but as we talked about in Chapter 3, you must apply the "Energy Pull Limit" rule. You cannot, by any means, mistreat or manipulate your energy by speaking negativity, living an unauthentic life, or starving your spirit. You have to treat your energy like you would treat your bank account and debit card, monitor it like it's your credit report, and lock it down like it's a high-value item that can only be housed in a vault with maximum security. I had to learn how to meditate and allow my energy to flow through me. My anxiety has improved since I learned how to ground my energy and incorporate the "Pulling of the energy" technique. Are you protecting your energy?

Self- Reflection:

1. Which ways do you need to start protecting your energy?
2. How will you apply the Energy Pull Limit?
3. What boundaries will you establish to protect your energy in the future?

Chapter 9

Triggers

Psalm 37: 8-9 (NIV) Refrain from anger and turn from wrath; do not fret it leads only to evil. For those who are evil will be destroyed, but those who hope in the Lord will inherit the land.

Triggers can be trauma-related or self-inflicted. Let me give you a quick breakdown of each one. Triggers are things that remind you of painful memories or symptoms of someone or something. Trauma triggers are psychological, causing you to recall past traumatic experiences and bring them to the present time, leading to feelings that affect your emotions and make your conscious-self react in an unhealthy way. Self-inflicted triggers are triggers from which you have healed, and you choose to go back and reflect on painful memories or things that no longer serve you, causing your healed self to start unraveling back to a state of being unhealed from a situation. Triggers can cause you to make poor judgments, leading to self-sabotage, and may prevent you from progressing toward your self-love journey. My triggers birthed my understanding of self-control. As we discussed in the previous chapter on self-control, I had to learn a gray area, but before I could understand the gray area, I had to identify and understand what was triggering me and why it triggered me. Like many of you, I had a lot of triggers, and I had to break them down and confront each one. I realized most of them started from my childhood. This was so deep for me that I had to go to therapy to help me prioritize them and disconnect from each one. I understood that I couldn't do it alone and reached out for help. Not all triggers can be self-healed; most of them are too intense once uncovered and will need mental health assistance to help you get to the root of the problem delicately. Once you start a healthier journey learning how to move on in life without past trauma affecting you, you will create healthier boundaries and understand the importance of why you shouldn't look back or allow people and things in your life that no longer serve you. You have to remember practicing bad habits of obsession can cause mental chaos for yourself. Do not be ashamed to seek professional help.

Self- Reflection:

1. Take a moment to reflect on the last confrontation or disagreement that could've caused a negative outcome.
2. Identify the emotions you felt before, during, and after that situation.
3. In the during phase, what caused your emotions to escalate?
4. If you identified what caused you to act out of emotions, then you just identified one of many of your triggers. Now that your trigger has been identified create a gray area and practice in the future.

Chapter 10

Obsession

Philippians 4:6 (NIV) Do not be anxious about anything, but in every situation, by prayer and petition, with thanksgiving, present your requests to God.

Obsession, in basic terms, is strong, impulsive thoughts. Obsession caused me anxiety, which led to my depression, impulsive thinking, and actions that were created from my unhealed mental creative space. I believe many people suffer from unhealed thinking that causes obsession. Obsession can look like many things: it can be an obsession with receiving love from someone else, future outcomes of situations, looking for signs from God, etc. Whatever it looks like, we need to understand it is not healthy and is conjured up by mixing your thoughts, memories, attachments, low self-esteem, and lack of self-love from an unhealed version of yourself and spoken over yourself like a spell that causes your mind to overreact. One of the many obsessions I had was looking for the blessings I knew were coming from God. I would be so much in my head, thinking, "How is it coming?" and asking God, "Where is it?" I can laugh about it now, but it was far from funny when I was going through it. I would cry, then get in my head and create doubt, which caused me to doubt God. That was bad business for me and caused God to teach me patience. We all know when the Most High has to sit us down to understand, He will put pressure on us heavily, but yet you will still feel His love and gentleness. Philippians 4:6 "Do not be anxious about anything." When I was operating in my unhealed headspace, I became discouraged, cried, and had so many pity parties. After those parties were over, my hangover consisted of self-inflicted stress, anxiety, depression, and confusion. I realized that some of my self-inflicted pain was the real root of my problems. Obsessing over what's next, instead of standing still in God, knowing He said, "Knock, and the door shall open." We have to stand strong on HIS word, pray, and let it go in faith, trusting that your ask or request will be done, unless it's not His will. But even then, with patience, you will see why His will is better.

Self-Reflection:

1. Reflect on the last time you obsessively thought about something.
2. Understanding obsession from a different perspective. Do you still feel that emotion when you reflect back on that obsessive thing?
3. How will you prevent obsessive thinking in the future?

Chapter 11

Self-Reflection

The Mirror You Reflect From

Self-reflection is the process of evaluating or reevaluating yourself. It allows you to look at your part in a situation and accept accountability for your actions without overthinking, as this can lead to guilt, shame, anxiety, or depression. When you start self-reflecting, it is very important not to obsess and trigger emotions that you create while reflecting on yourself or the situation. A healthy way for me to reflect is not by dwelling on a situation but by checking myself truthfully about how I approached a situation. If I feel I am at fault, then I release it, apologize if I'm able to, and aim to do better next time. I also try to see things from others' points of view without absorbing the situation and changing my values to fit theirs. We have to be understanding and never push our agenda on anyone. While in this phase, I am able to accept what is and discard what does not serve me during my healing process. This phase has taught me that all negative things that happen are not happening to me but for me. I take it as a learning experience, and the outcome has taught me to handle bad situations graciously and stop judging myself or others. I approach all situations with a self-less approach in order to maintain my balance but making sure I protect my energy by transmuting the negative energy. Starting today, how will you start to view yourself through the mirror you reflect from?

Self-Reflection:

1. Think back to the last situation that may have caused you to act out of character or irritate your peace.
2. Do you still hold negative emotions towards that situation?
3. If you are still holding an emotion towards that "person, place, or thing," try viewing it from someone else's point of view. Reflect on your part and see if it could have had a different outcome if you handled it from a healthy mental space.
4. List some ways practicing self-reflection could help you with future situations.

Chapter 12

Transmuting Energy

Psalm 35: 26 NIV May all who gloat over my distress be put to shame and confusion; may all who exalt themselves over me be clothed with shame and disgrace.

Transmutation means to change, and transmuting energy means shifting something from negative to positive. In the previous chapter, we talked about grounding our energy. The first thing you should do before grounding your energy is to identify your emotions. Identifying your emotions involves acknowledging what you are feeling and trying to put a name to it (for example, if you are feeling sad, then identify it as sad and not as mad or angry). This step will help you understand how energy can be manipulated. Manipulating energy is when you go from feeling good to suddenly feeling the opposite when you get around someone, a place, or a thing. This can also have a positive effect because you can feel down, and someone can come near you, and your energy changes to positive, so it is not always bad. We are all made up of energy; energy is all around us, and we can't stop it, but what we can do is understand how to manage it. I manage and transmute energy in a couple of ways. One way is to pray over it because whatever the enemy meant for bad God can turn it into good. Another way is to meditate on it and release all negative energy by focusing on positive energy. Also, self-reflecting is a good way to identify if your energy is being manipulated. This process healed me in my journey because it allowed me to recognize my emotions and remove myself from places, things, or people when I felt the energy shift. I found myself with a smaller circle of friends, distancing myself from certain family members and releasing all the things I didn't want to be with me on the other side of my journey. Friends, remember you are in control of your energy and have to make the right choices to live a peaceful, self-loved life. Call back all your energy and stand in your power as the powerful warrior that God created you to be.

Self-Reflection:

1. I want you to think of times when you felt your energy was manipulated.
2. Thinking back to those times, can you identify now what caused your energy shift?
3. How can you mitigate this from happening in the future?

Chapter 13

Meditation

Philippians 4:8 Finally, brothers and sisters, whatever is true, whatever is noble, whatever is right, whatever is pure, whatever is lovely, whatever is admirable—if anything is excellent or praiseworthy—think about such things.

This is the chapter where you can pull all the other chapters together to start your self-love healing journey. Most people think meditating is hard or boring, but it is the opposite. This is a time for you to go within, get clarity about yourself, and start creating a new you just by imagining it. That is how simple it is: you create what you want your life to be. This is a no-judgment zone where you can be honest with yourself and not worry about anyone else's feelings but your own. Meditation is to focus your mind for a period of time or think deeply about something. There's no right or wrong way to position yourself or your setting as long as you are comfortable and in a safe place. You have to find what works for you because you are different from the next person. There are plenty of beneficial reasons why you should meditate. I meditate for clarity and to rebalance my energy to help me hear God's voice clearer and reflect on situations in a healthy way. In doing this, I am able to identify my own energy and transmute all negative energy or disregard it. Meditation is a healthy way to ponder a specific thing without obsessing over it but thinking about ways to solve, end, or understand that "thing" you are deeply thinking about. Philippians 4:8 reminds me to think about good things when I meditate, which causes me to exude positive energy. I started using guided meditation and then started making my own techniques. The benefit of meditation is that it teaches you how to sit quietly and embrace the stillness while your mind adventures off on other things. The key is to grab your thoughts and recenter by taking a deep breath in and blowing out slowly, causing you to focus on your breathing. Don't worry if you can't concentrate, because some days I can't, but I allow myself to feel whatever emotion is going on with me, and I acknowledge and process what belongs to me and disregard what doesn't. This practice is not once and done; you should make it a part of your routine. Try sitting quietly for 5 minutes while taking deep breaths and blowing out slowly, and tell yourself, *"I love you."*

Self-Reflection:

1. Today, I want you to create a safe place to start your meditation.
2. Create a playlist of soft music or sounds that can help you while in meditation.
3. How will you incorporate this practice into your routine while on your journey?

Chapter 14

Conclusion

Birthing A New You

We have finally made it to the end of my personal trinity walk to self-love that helped me heal during this journey. This doesn't have to be the end of yours; you can personalize your journey to fit you. I only suggest that you go to God and ask Him for clarity on your purpose so you can align yourself while you embark on your journey. Also, don't be afraid to reach out for professional help because most of our problems start from childhood wounds. Getting to the root of most problems may require you to go deep within and heal your inner child. As a child, you didn't know how to protect your energy or even understand that it was an actual thing. My experience wasn't easy, but through God, I was able to go inward and heal. Once I started healing, I learned to let go of all things that were attached to my inner child. The child in me was bullied and balled up in a corner, frightened and too afraid to speak or cry. I had to go back and comfort her gently with kindness. Releasing that hurt started with me hugging, loving, and speaking life over myself. Once I started healing (I cried for days over the childhood pain, but in those moments of healing, I birthed a new thing). I looked in the mirror and told her it was time to let go, and she would be safe because I was you. "You go play and enjoy being a kid because you should've never had to endure the pain that was inflicted on you as a child." I felt true joy, and everything I looked for people to do for me, I started doing for myself. This allowed me to give birth to the new me, and I call her "Maliha" (Ma-lee-ha), meaning queen, beloved, beauty, and strength. Operating in my new power and authority, I started treating myself kinder and very gently, like a newborn. Life looked a little different; my walk became more confident, my speech became clearer, and I had a boldness about myself. I embodied my new name and became slow to speak or angry. Taking my place and aligning with God allowed Him to carry me like a Father would his daughter. He began to show me what real love from other people looks and feels like. Letting go and letting God, I was able to enjoy life like a child. I was able to have real joy, laughter, and carefreeness, knowing that I was protected by the Most High. I started making wishes like a child, asking God for the impossible and receiving it without worry. I was able to manifest a whole new life for myself because I believed and trusted Him. My testimony is not just for me but for me to share with you. I am sharing my Trinity Walk to Self-Love with you, hoping it will help guide you in creating your own journey. Remember to speak your truth; you may see things one way, and someone else may view them another way, and that is okay. You just stand on your truth and focus on your path to becoming a healed version of yourself.

Self-Reflection:

1. Reflecting back to Chapter 1 question "How do you define self-love?" Now that you have a full understanding of the Trinity Walk to Self- Love. Do you define self- love differently?
2. What will your new name be?

Understanding Meditation

The first-time people try meditating, they will do what they see. They will sit with their legs folded like a pretzel, lie down, play soft jazz music, loud music, quiet music, etc. Once they realize that their minds are drifting away, they open their eyes and say, "This is not working," "I can't do this," or, "It's boring," and quit. Your mind is doing exactly what it is supposed to do, so don't quit just yet; you have to practice. I will teach you my technique, and then you can create techniques that fit you.

Create a safe, comfortable place. You can play soft music if needed and sit or lie comfortably. Close your eyes and focus on your inner self. Start with focusing on your breathing, breathing in, and slowly blowing out. Now, start at the top of your head, all the way down to your feet, focusing on each muscle and relaxing that muscle. You will then recognize how much tension you have been putting on your muscle groups. For example, focus on your forehead area and tell your mind to relax the muscles in your forehead. You'd be surprised how tense the muscles in your face are. Do this for your entire body. Remember, everything starts inside. After you relax your muscles, focus on your mind. Your mind will wander off, and that is okay. Let your mind roam freely without you forcing it in a direction. Your job is to learn to release control because your mind knows it's in a safe place where you don't have to be on guard. If your mind starts to guide into negative thinking, or you start controlling your mind, then you grab those thoughts, refocus back to the start position of where your meditation first started, which is your breathing, and then repeat if necessary.

STAY CONNECTED

BODYBYNIFITNESS@GMAIL.COM

www.nifitnessllc.com

www.ingramcontent.com/pod-product-compliance
Lightning Source LLC
Chambersburg PA
CBHW040847120626
46547CB00001B/57